Ghosts and Gold

Ghosts and Gold

My Story of Ghost Ranch

Keith Dean Myers

GHOSTS AND GOLD: My Story of Ghost Ranch. Copyright 2020 by Keith Dean Myers. All rights reserved. Printed in the United States of America. No part of this book may be used or reproduced in any manner whatsoever without written permission, other than in the case of brief quotations embodied in critical articles and reviews. For information contact: Keith Dean Myers, kdmoffice3519@earthlink.net.

FIRST EDITION 2020

Ghosts and Gold: My Story of Ghost Ranch
Myers, Keith Dean
Photos by Keith Dean Myers
Edited by Helen Rynaski
Design by Wink Visual Arts

ISBN 978-0-578-67186-4

For our granddaughters, Robin and Keira Brown,
who are growing up loving and respecting
our beautiful home planet.

As a person who has been haunted and variously awakened by the beauty and mysteries of Ghost Ranch, I applaud this book and its invitation to let stories live beyond their particulars. The history of such a culturally complex place adds to its ongoing richness. "Don't bury the gold," Myers says. "Share it, let it shine."

— Jane Vincent Taylor teaches poetry at Ghost Ranch. She lives, writes, teaches, and makes art in Oklahoma. janevincenttaylor.blogspot.com

Dean Myers' deep love of place truly shines through in Ghosts and Gold. If you love Ghost Ranch too, this is the perfect book for the whole family!

— Sean Murphy, National Endowment for the Arts Fellow, author of *The Time of New Weather*

Contents

Acknowledgments ix

Prologue 1

1. In the Valley of Shining Stone 3

2. History Before Written Records.......................... 10

3. The Written Story Begins 15

4. Cattle Thieves at Rancho de los Brujos 18

5. Escape to Freedom 20

6. Today's Ghost Ranch is Born 23

7. The Past Returns, and is Still Present 27

8. The Spirit of Today's Ghost Ranch 32

9. The Spirit of Ghost Ranch in Me 35

Suggested Reading 37

The Author 39

Acknowledgments

This book began more than a decade ago as a ghost story told to a gathering of church families at a Halloween party. It has slowly grown into a more complete account of Ghost Ranch, yet it remains a first-person narrative built upon my experiences, understandings, and feelings. Nearly all of the photographs are mine.

I am deeply grateful to the following people for their wisdom and encouragement: Ghost Ranch Executive Director Paul Fogg offered support on behalf of the ranch and permission to include my photos in this book. *Ghosts and Gold* is a small token of my gratitude to Ghost Ranch. Ghost Ranch Writers' Workshop leaders Ina Hughes, Sean Murphy, Anita Skeen, and Jane Taylor started me on my writing journey, and have continued to mentor and challenge me. Particular thanks go to Sean and Jane for carefully reviewing early drafts and offering thoughtful suggestions for improvements. Douglas Dunn and Lee Hall of the Cleveland Museum of Natural History provided informed suggestions regarding the geology and paleontology sections. Helen Rynaski helpfully edited later drafts, and Kelly Pasholk of Wink Visual Arts performed outstanding design services.

Finally, I am personally grateful to my wife, Maxine, and to our daughters, Elizabeth Brown (and her husband, Jonathan) and Rebecca Myers, for their patience and understanding throughout this book's long gestation.

And I thank you for reading and listening to my story of Ghost Ranch. I hope that one day, if you have not done so already, you will be able to experience and share your own Ghost Ranch story.

— Dean Myers

Prologue

The young mother walks cautiously beside the small burro, balancing her little girl on its back as it picks its way along the rocky trail. She does not dare let the child slide off the sure-footed animal. The cold desert night threatens to make every step their last. The moon and the stars are their only light. But they must keep going. Their lives depend on it.

A nighttime escape attempt across northern New Mexico's high desert by a mother and child and small burro is unlikely to free them from this enormous land's clutches. Even on a clear night, when moonlight and starlight punctuate the black sky, it is risky for them to make their way on trails strewn with rocks and studded with exposed roots. Shadows play games with everything they see. The young woman or the burro might trip over something on the trail and tumble helplessly down a rock-strewn slope into a deep ravine. A broken leg would stop their travel altogether. And although they will welcome the light of a new day, the mother knows that same light will make it easier for her husband's murderer to find them.

She has to stay alert for any wild animal that might stalk them. She shudders at every sound she hears coming out of the night — the snap of a branch, the rumble of a falling rock, the growl — or even just the breathing — of some other living thing.

But little frightens the mother more than the tales of spirits and monsters she is sure live in this desert. Even though she fears she will not be able to overpower them, she has to be ready to defend herself and her child. She knows they are out there.

If her husband's killer or a wild beast does not catch them, one of the ghostly creatures living in the canyons at the base of the soaring rock cliffs very well might. Mother and daughter must get to the safety of Ohkay Owingeh Pueblo, her family home. They must escape from a place they know as Rancho de los Brujos (The Witches' Ranch), a place now called Ghost Ranch.

CLIFFS SURROUNDING GHOST RANCH CAMPUS

1.
In the Valley of Shining Stone

Come with me to northern New Mexico, and I will tell you about Ghost Ranch's ghosts, creatures, and people. I will tell you tales of a beautiful place that I love.

The towering red, white, and yellow cliffs that embrace Ghost Ranch are visible from miles away. They loom ever higher over you as your car bounces down the dusty lane that leads to the cluster of buildings at the core of life here. You feel as if the 600 and 700-foot rock walls — nearly as high as a 60-story building — could overpower you and hold you in their grasp forever. They have captured me and will not let go.

Tiny pieces of quartz embedded in the massive stone walls reflect bright sunlight and even pale moonlight, so early Spanish explorers named the desert valley they guard Piedra Lumbre (Valley of Shining Stone).

Ghost Ranch itself occupies about 21,000 acres of the Piedra Lumbre, fanning out to the southwest from the base of the cliffs. If you could fit those acres into a square, each side would be over five and a half miles long. But its boundaries are very irregular because of the surrounding cliffs, hills, and canyons.

The ranch's red dirt is a fine dust that is easily blown about by the wind when it is dry. When wet, it sticks to your shoes and to everything else. When it is pressed together and dries again, it feels hard as rock. Scrape that hard surface and you release red dust. Adobe bricks for building can be made from the ground you walk on at Ghost Ranch.

TRAIL TOWARD BOX CANYON

Trees, bushes, and cacti — often growing in isolation — populate Ghost Ranch. Small rodents, reptiles, insects, and spiders that survive on little water skitter here and there among these plants. You might even see larger animals, such as bobcats and coyotes. This desert does not look like the Sahara, where there is only sand for miles on end. New Mexico's high desert is home to a surprising number of living things, large and small.

Ghost Ranch gets very little rain and a tiny bit of snow each year, less than ten inches of water, all told. But a stream called the

Rito del Yeso (The Little River of the Gypsum) flows out of Box Canyon at the north end of the ranch. The banks of the Rito del Yeso are green with grasses, shrubs, and trees, attracting both animals and human beings.

Where does that water come from? The upper end of Box Canyon narrows until fifty-foot-high rock walls on the right and the left curve around and meet to form a giant letter U. The base of these curved walls is wet with the water of underground streams seeping out of the rock. Here is the source of the Rito del Yeso.

RITO DEL YESO

From that point, the boulder-filled stream winds down Box Canyon. Most of the time the Rito del Yeso is quite small, but an afternoon thunderstorm can cause it to swell and rise in a flash, sweeping away everything in its path. Just such a storm happened in 2015, and crashing, rushing water instantly re-arranged the landscape. Trees, bushes, the ranch's irrigation system, pottery shed and kilns, and several other buildings were destroyed and carried far downstream in a matter of moments. Fortunately, no human lives were lost, though surely many animals died that afternoon.

Box Canyon widens into the Piedra Lumbre valley. There, before that destructive storm, the Rito del Yeso irrigated Ghost Ranch's fields and gardens. Today, deep wells provide water for human use, but the Rito del Yeso is the ancient heart of Ghost Ranch.

The horizon south of Ghost Ranch is dominated by a distinctive mountain whose peak looks like a black blade slicing into the blue sky. This mountain's steep flanks are loaded with a very hard kind of flint, which is why the Spanish named it Cerro Pedernal, Spanish for "flint hill." For many generations before

CERRO PEDERNAL

CHIMNEY ROCK

the Spaniards' arrival, it was a prime source of materials for tools and weapons, and the native people considered Cerro Pedernal a sacred site. Even today, people regard it with awe.

Chimney Rock is a gigantic rock tower to the northwest of the ranch that looks like its name, and is often photographed and painted. Many hikers follow the trail that leads to the cliff that overlooks it. A longer and more difficult hike takes you to the top of Kitchen Mesa, east of the ranch. From the top of either, you can see the whole extent of the ranch and the vast landscape beyond.

During the day, Ghost Ranch offers challenging adventures in a wild land. Nights are even more challenging. It is inky dark up here when the sun goes down and the moon is in hiding, or merely a silvery sliver. Even the millions of stars in the black sky

— more stars than you ever imagined because there are few human-made lights to block their light — are not much help.

People believe ghosts inhabit many parts of New Mexico. Communities throughout the state claim to be home to spooky, powerful spirits. So, why is this particular place in northern New Mexico called Ghost Ranch?

CHOLLA FAMILY

Because Ghost Ranch's history and landscape breathe life into such stories, and those stories haunt me when I am there. More than a century after the woman and child fled from Rancho de los Brujos, I cannot be at Ghost Ranch without feeling its spirits and its beasts. I imagine ghostly figures darting up and down the sheer rock walls, riding the currents of the wind with ravens, hawks, and vultures. I see witches lurking among tree trunks and scrub bushes and boulders at the bottoms of the shadowy canyons that cut through the cliffs and open into the valley. I picture specters roosting in the tops of cottonwoods along the arroyos, or in the scraggly, half-dead skeletons of junipers. In my mind I conjure small shades taking the form of the cholla, so that at night, in the moon's glow, the thorny limbs of that innocent cactus look like arms groping toward the sky.

When I walk the trails of Ghost Ranch, I wonder what cunning ghost might transform itself into a scorpion, rattlesnake, or tarantula, and then glide and slide across the desert floor until it gets so close to me I feel its icy breath on my toes.

I never let down my guard, even in bright daylight. I know Ghost Ranch's many risks to my safety, despite its beauties. And I remember a dear friend — devoted to Ghost Ranch — who lost his life in a tragic accident while hiking among the massive cliffs.

2

History Before Written Records

The story of planet Earth began billions of years ago. The story of the Ghost Ranch that you can visit today began far more recently, during what is called the Triassic Period, around 220 million years ago. That is the age of the oldest rocks at the base of the cliffs.

Over the course of those millions of years, powerful forces deep in the earth pushed up massive sections of land and shifted them around. Sometimes, this land was covered with seas and lakes; other times, it was exposed to the air, with streams and rivers flowing through it. Wind and water deposited minerals and other sediments onto the land, often of different colors and consistencies. As these deposits built up, the older, lower levels were pressed into rock by the weight of the newer levels on top of them.

When the land was not covered by seas, rushing rivers and howling winds sculpted it into ever new shapes. Fast-moving water carved canyons and valleys deep into the rock, starting with the top layer and working its way down into older layers. The newly exposed rock was then subject to sand- and grit-carrying winds that constantly altered its appearance.

At the same time, the climate slowly changed. Areas that were once wet and green became dry and brown, and then turned again. And living things — plants and animals and other organisms — continued their parade through time, both shaping and being shaped by their environments.

ROCK FORMATION NEAR TRAIL TO BOX CANYON

There is evidence of life in the oldest layers we can see at Ghost Ranch. One of the creatures that lived here around 200 million years ago was an early dinosaur named *Coelophysis bauri*, or simply, *Coelophysis*. At that time, this land's warm and damp climate hosted a forest of soaring pine trees. It was located much nearer Earth's equator than it is today, having been moved to where it is now by the slow creep of tectonic plates.

Coelophysis was a light-weight, slender animal that could be nearly ten feet long from the end of its nose to the tip of its tail. *Coelophysis* means "hollow form." It was named that because of its hollow bones. It stood and ran very fast on two large hind legs, and used its smaller front legs to grasp and hold prey. *Coelophysis* was a voracious carnivore.

But, unlike later and much larger dinosaurs, *Coelophysis* was not at the top of the food chain. That honor may have belonged to members of at least two kinds of huge reptiles. Mostly aquatic phytosaurs, which may have grown to as long as twenty feet, looked and probably acted much like very large crocodiles. Nearly thirty-foot-long rauisuchians also looked a bit like crocs, but had longer legs and wider snouts. These enormous beasts could dine on *Coelophysis bauri* — when they could catch one.

When prehistoric animals died, their bodies and bones were often covered by layers of sediments (mud, silt, sand, pebbles, etc.) deposited by the winds that blew around them and the water that flowed over them. Mineral-saturated groundwater gradually penetrated the bones, filling or replacing them with minerals such as quartz and calcite. As layers of sediment deposits built up one on top of another, the lower, older layers were compressed into rock, entombing the fossilized bones. All this took millions of years.

Human beings appeared in what is now northern New Mexico at least 13,000 years ago. Large mammals such as mammoths, camels, horses, and bison thrived at the time because the cooler climate made the area good for grasses. The earliest humans hunted animals and harvested seeds and roots of plants to provide food for themselves. As the centuries passed, the people who came after them learned to domesticate some animals (such as turkeys and ducks) and to grow corn, beans, and pumpkins. That was the beginning of agriculture.

About 900 years ago people from the west moved into the area along the Rio Grande, north of present-day Santa Fe. They built their villages out of adobe and stone. Their family living spaces were connected to one another, sometimes stacked two or three stories high, so that they looked like apartment buildings. The Spanish who later came to the area called these villages "pueblos." Descendants of these early pueblo nations are the dominant Native American residents of this part of New Mexico to this day.

ROCK ART

Some still live in pueblos very similar to those of their ancestors.

Many of the different pueblo nations spoke similar, but distinctive, languages from a common origin. Six of them — including Ohkay Owingeh — spoke (and still speak) a language called Tewa. But none of them left written records of their time here. They carved pictures of the world they knew on rocks, and many of the stories they told continue to be passed down through the generations. People today study those carvings and listen closely to those stories. They also examine remains of buildings and analyze bones, pottery, and other evidence. In these ways we learn how early peoples lived, worked, and thought, how they dressed and what they ate, and much more.

Northern New Mexico's landscape opens a window onto ancient transformations of our planet and the evolution of life itself. Unlike flatlands and lands covered with thick vegetation, here you can easily see evidence of the processes of creation.

HISTORY BEFORE WRITTEN RECORDS

Sometimes, when I stand upon Ghost Ranch's red earth and open my senses to everything around me, I feel as if the past and I are watching each other — as if long-ago ages are inviting me to look and listen and learn from what they want to teach me. The Valley of Shining Stone's ancient story is a spirit who whispers in my ear, *Pay attention and you will see planet Earth as you have never seen her before.*

CHIMNEY ROCK IN THE MORNING SUN

3.

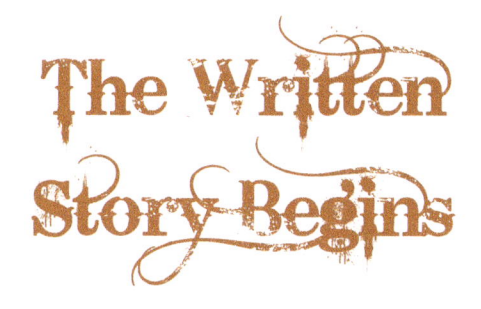

The Written Story Begins

Around 500 years ago, explorers from Spain entered what is now the southwestern United States. They came here because they had heard they would find gold, and they brought armies to make the gold and the land their own. They left the first written records of the area.

The people already living here fought hard and bravely to keep their homeland for themselves and their families. But, eventually, the Spanish conquered the area by threatening, moving, and often killing the native inhabitants.

These conquerors also brought the Christian faith to the land's peoples, sometimes forcing them to follow it. Old churches and Spanish place names that dot the southwestern landscape are reminders of those early Europeans' presence.

Despite the Spaniards' efforts, they did not find gold.

In 1821, Mexico — which then included all or parts of present-day California, New Mexico, Arizona, Colorado, Utah, and Nevada — became independent from Spain. A little more than twenty-five years later, following the Mexican-American War of 1846 to 1848, the United States claimed the New Mexico

Territory — the current states and parts of states I just mentioned — as its own. In 1912, a portion of this territory became the 47th state, New Mexico.

The United States government continued to try to control the descendants of the original peoples of the land, called Indians by most white Americans. Our government forced the children of these indigenous inhabitants to attend schools where only English was spoken. It also tried to prevent them from practicing time-honored cultural and religious traditions. Such policies have changed in recent years, but because of discrimination and poverty, life is still very difficult for many of the native people who live on and near the reservations set aside for them.

Today, northern New Mexico, including the area around Ghost Ranch, is home to a rich mix of native peoples and the descendants of immigrants who moved here from Spain, Mexico, and other parts of the United States. It is also home to newer residents from many lands and cultures.

That is a lot of information. But it is important to the entire story I am about to tell you of how Ghost Ranch became what it is today. It is the setting for the story of the escaping mother and daughter. She knew the rocks and the cliffs, the canyons and the valleys, though she probably had little sense of how they had been shaped by nature's forces over millions of years. She knew how to survive the harsh environment. She knew about the many peoples who lived together in her homeland, even if not always in peace. Most of all, this mother knew that only she could save her child from certain death in the desert.

GOLDEN TREES

4.

Cattle Thieves at Rancho de los Brujos

Ghosts can live anywhere, but one place they always live is in people's imaginations. People often think they hear or see or feel ghosts in lonely, dark places. And people like to make other people think there are ghosts around — as when you sneak up behind your friend and shout, "BOO!"

Back in the 1880s, two men — Juan Ignacio Archuleta and his younger brother (whose name I do not know) — scared people with stories of ghosts at their little homestead on the Rito del Yeso. These Archuletas were members of a family that was a mix of native, Mexican, and Spanish peoples of the area.

The brothers tried to frighten people away from their place because they were cattle thieves. They stole cows from neighboring ranchers and hid them at their own ranch until they could sell them to other neighbors or in the markets around Santa Fe. They made enough money selling other peoples' cattle to support themselves and their gang of henchmen. They were so feared that sometimes people called them Los Animales — the animals.

The Archuletas hid the stolen livestock part way up Box Canyon, along the Rito del Yeso. There, they built a corral to contain the cattle that actually belonged to their neighbors. For themselves, the brothers built crude wood and mud stockade-type houses, not far from the wide opening of Box Canyon. They lived in these "jacal" houses, which were also not visible from the distant dirt road. Travelers could not see the ranch's buildings, nor could they hear the bellowing cattle.

But Juan and his brother wanted to make sure no one would ever come into their ranch. That is why they told stories about scary things living there. They may have heard some of the stories from others, and some they may have made up.

The stories they told were not just about witches and ghosts, but about strange creatures such as "earth babies" — six feet long and covered with red hair — that wailed and moaned their way out of the ground at night. And tales of a winged cow that swooped down the canyons to warn of coming sickness and death. Most horrible of all were stories of Vivaron. Vivaron was chief of the evil spirits, a thirty-foot-long creature that ate human flesh. It was said to look like a snake.

When the wind howled and darkness fell, and moonlight played upon the steep cliff walls, it took little imagination to fear that, at any moment, a frightening figure might swoop out of the dark to nibble on your ears, all the time filling them with its screeches and howls.

You can be sure that few outsiders strayed onto the Archuletas' land. Unsuspecting passersby, who somehow found the ranch and stopped there expecting hospitality, were rarely seen again. But their horses and saddles often showed up in the Santa Fe market months later. No one dared go where people said ghosts and huge blood-thirsty creatures lived, and where they claimed bodies were buried in wells or just cut into pieces and scattered on the dry ground of the Valley of Shining Stone.

5.

Escape to Freedom

The younger Archuleta brother took a woman from Ohkay Owingeh for his wife. Ohkay Owingeh, in the Tewa language, means "Place of the Strong People." The Spanish had named it San Juan Pueblo, and that is what it is called in older books and maps. It is south of Ghost Ranch and just north of the town of Española.

We do not know how the couple met or if she came willingly with him to Rancho de los Brujos. But we do know that, in time, the woman gave birth to a daughter.

One day her husband drove a herd of stolen cattle to Santa Fe to sell them. When he returned to Ghost Ranch he told his brother, Juan, that he had buried the gold he had received in payment for the cows in the nearby hills. Perhaps he told him that he wanted to hide it from thieves, or maybe even from their own hired hands.

Juan did not trust his younger brother. Did he suspect that the younger Archeleta wanted to keep more than his share of the gold, or perhaps that he had lost it all in a poker game? In a fit of rage, Juan hacked his brother to death with an axe. That is often the way of thieves, even if they are brothers.

The murderer was sure that his brother's wife — now his widow — knew where the gold was. Juan threatened that if she did not lead him to the gold by the next day he would feed her child to Vivaron, who liked young flesh best of all. Then he left her alone in her house. *She won't dare go anywhere*, the thief and murderer may have thought as he drifted off into sleep.

COTTONWOOD TREES AND RESTORED JACAL HOUSE

Ghost Ranch can be a very disorienting place. The towering cliffs, the rambling hills, the harsh and spare desert — you can get turned around even if you keep focused and clear-eyed at all times. A woman and small burro could easily become hopelessly lost here at night, if some awful creature did not seize them first. There are more things to fear here than one person can ever see.

But with the life of her young daughter at stake, this mother could not let fear stop her. In the middle of the night she arose. In the cool air she led a burro out of the corral and lifted the child onto the trusting animal's back. Then the three of them plunged into the dark desert. They skirted the bases of the great cliffs and made their way among the silent, watching cholla and junipers.

We will never know the route they took, but the woman surely knew she had to reach the canyon through which the Chama River plunges into the wide Chama River Valley. From there, it would be a relatively easy journey home to Ohkay Owingeh, and to welcome and safety for her, for her daughter, and for the burro. Home was the only clear thing in her sight as she pressed forward. Any way home was difficult and dangerous, scattered with rocks and roots, watched by unseen creatures.

The mother relaxed just a bit when they reached the more level path on the verdant Chama Valley floor. Finally, the three of them arrived, certainly exhausted and hungry, at her pueblo and family at Ohkay Owingeh. They had traveled at least forty miles.

Word soon got out that Juan Archuleta had killed his brother, and that many of the hired men had fled. Even they were afraid to live and work at the haunted ranch, and with a man who had murdered his own brother. An angry mob of neighbors attacked the rustlers' homestead. Juan himself escaped, but some of his remaining cowboys were hanged from the high branches of a giant cottonwood tree just outside the door of one of the jacal houses.

The ranch at the mouth of Box Canyon, in the valley watered by the Rito del Yeso, was abandoned for twenty years. No one was brave enough to live here, so fearful were they of the spirits and specters they were sure hovered in and around Box Canyon. The terrifying stories of witches and ghosts, and of grisly murders, kept people far from the buildings and corrals near the canyon's opening.

6.
Today's Ghost Ranch is Born

Several people laid claim to Rancho de los Brujos during the early years of the 20th century until, in 1927 or 1928, a man named Roy Pfaffle won it in a card game. Or so the story goes. No one knows for sure what happened.

When Pfaffle brought home his newly won deed to Rancho de los Brujos, he gave it to his wife, Carol Bishop Stanley. In 1929, she took that deed to the courthouse and registered the property in her name alone. Two years later, after she and Roy Pfaffle divorced, Stanley moved to her property on the Ranch of the Witches. Only one of the Archuletas' jacal houses was still standing, and it took a lot of work to make it livable. But Stanley was a determined woman. She fixed up the old house and moved in, even bringing with her the Steinway grand piano she loved to play.

Carol Stanley's persistence and hard work started Rancho de los Brujos on the path to what it is today. She built new housing and invited guests to the place she called Ghost Ranch. She turned the one-time rustlers' hideout into a guest ranch (sometimes called a dude ranch), a place to which people would travel to try out life in the Old West for a few days or weeks. Well-off and adventurous families paid to stay at Stanley's place in the high desert, and she provided them with rooms, food, and activities such as horseback riding so they could feel close to the desert and its inhabitants.

In 1933, Arthur Pack, from New Jersey, brought his wife and children to Ghost Ranch, hoping the dry climate would be good for his daughter's pneumonia. Pack was a writer and the editor of *Nature* magazine. He deeply loved and respected the New Mexico high desert lands. He was also fairly well-off financially. After one night at Ghost Ranch, sleeping outside under the great cottonwood trees near the restored jacal house, he decided this would be his family's new home. He negotiated and bought a plot of ranch land from Stanley, and there, a few miles west of the main Ghost Ranch campus, the Pack family built a house for themselves. They called it Rancho de los Burros — Ranch of the Burros.

Just after the Pack's first visit to Ghost Ranch, famous Chicago architect Edward Bennett traveled there with his son. He was so enthralled with the ranch that he bought land not far from the Pack family's Rancho de los Burros and built his family's summer home there. He called it Casa Monte Rojo — the Red Hill House.

Robert and Seward Johnson, heirs to the Johnson & Johnson pharmaceutical company, liked Ghost Ranch so much that, in 1935, they built a home (designed by Edward Bennett, and the only two-story building on the ranch) for their family visits.

Managing a guest ranch is expensive and difficult, and even with guests like the Bennetts and the Johnsons, Carol Stanley's Ghost Ranch struggled financially. To make matters worse, during the 1930s, the world suffered from the Great Depression. Few Americans had extra money to spend, and trips to distant places like New Mexico were out of the question for most people. Stanley could not keep up with the cost of running the ranch and, in 1935, Arthur Pack bought all of it from her.

PEDERNAL IN WINTER

The Depression continued, only to be followed by World War II, but changes came to make it much easier for people to visit Ghost Ranch. It became increasingly accessible and comfortable because of electricity, refrigeration, the automobile, and the airplane. Pack invested money in Ghost Ranch and improved it to make it more inviting, while keeping it rustic and simple. Travel to and from the rustlers' old den was still difficult, and the vast desert still threatened, but enough guests came to the ranch to keep it operating.

Among Ghost Ranch's famous guests during these years were aviator Charles Lindbergh and his wife, Anne; photographer Ansel Adams; and orchestra conductor Leopold Stokowski.

The famous person whose name will always be associated with Ghost Ranch is Georgia O'Keeffe, one of the first well-known women painters. In the mid-1930s, after several summers of being a guest, she made Ghost Ranch and nearby Abiquiú her year-round home. In 1940, she bought Rancho de los Burros from Pack.

O'Keeffe painted what she saw and felt when she gazed at the deep blue sky, the red and gold hills, and the shining stone cliffs. Her paintings are in art museums around the world, and a museum in Santa Fe is devoted exclusively to her work. She was particularly fond of painting Cerro Pedernal, even claiming that God told her that if she painted it often enough, God would give it to her. She died in 1986, when she was 98 years old, but Cerro Pedernal continues to cast its spell on the Piedra Lumbre and Ghost Ranch.

O'Keeffe's painting of a cow skull has become the most familiar symbol of Ghost Ranch. It is her gift to the place she loved deeply, and it welcomes you as you pass through the main gate.

During World War II, in the early 1940s, Ghost Ranch hosted guests who revealed almost nothing about who they were and where they came from. Rumors were in the air about a secret government project at nearby Los Alamos National Laboratory. Only after the war did the ranch staff learn that the workers at Los Alamos had been developing the atom bomb. They and their families had come to the ranch to take a break from the stress of work. Ghost Ranch holds more than its share of mysteries and secrets!

7.
The Past Returns, and is Still Present

In 1966, Arthur Pack wrote a book titled *We Called It Ghost Ranch*. In it, he tells about the return to Ghost Ranch of two of the characters in the old story of the courageous nighttime escape by a woman, her young daughter, and a burro.

One of Pack's ranch hands was a man named Amarante Archuleta. He was a loyal and valued employee. Because Archuleta was, and is, a very common last name in northern New Mexico, the Packs may not have thought about any relationship to the two brothers who were cattle thieves. Or perhaps, because he was a good man, they did think about it but did not care.

Early one morning, an elderly, nearly blind man rode into the ranch calling, "Señor Paque, Señor Paque." He sounded very agitated, and Pack rushed out to meet him. The old man said his wife had died, and that Pack, as his son's employer, was responsible for her burial expenses. This was the custom at that time.

That old man turned out to be Juan Archuleta, the man who had murdered his own brother! Why had this criminal gone free all those years? We do not know, but that is the story Arthur Pack tells. In any case, Pack had his carpenter build a casket for Juan

Archuleta's wife (Amarante's mother), and he helped arrange for her funeral and burial near where Juan lived.

The second visitor from the past that Pack writes about was an older woman who rode into Ghost Ranch, and told him that she was the child who had been taken by her mother to the safety of Ohkay Owingeh. Now, she was back to look for the gold she believed her father had buried in the hills around the old jacal house. Perhaps she thought she could claim it as her own. While she was there, she told Pack stories of the frightening creatures that she was sure still lived at the ranch. Although she looked and looked for the buried gold, she did not find it. To this day, no one knows what happened to it.

The earliest inhabitants of Ghost Ranch to appear in modern times are *Coelophysis* and *Vivaron*.

In the late 1940s, an enormous jumble of fossilized *Coelophysis bauri* skeletons, tangled and embedded in solid rock, was discovered at Ghost Ranch, not far from where Box Canyon widens into the green valley the Rito del Yeso waters. The ancient creatures may have perished in a flash flood like the one that roared down Box Canyon in 2015. Paleontologists cut huge blocks of rock and fossils out of the ground and shipped them to museums all over the world for study, but they left one block at Ghost Ranch. It was moved several miles to a site near the ranch's buildings, where a beautiful museum was built around it. You can view it there today and try to count all the bones it reveals.

In 2002, archeologist and long-time Ghost Ranch associate and friend, John Hayden, was leading a tour of the ranch lands when he suggested that his party look for fossils of dinosaur bones at a particular location. To his great surprise, they found some. In time, paleontologists determined that some fossils found at what is now called the Hayden Quarry belonged to a previously unknown species of rauisuchian. This new-to-science species has been named after the most fearsome creature that the Archuleta brothers claimed stalked Ghost Ranch and after the man who led to its discovery — *Vivaron haydeni*. One way or another, Vivaron was and is here!

COELOPHYSIS BLOCK [CLEVELAND MUSEUM OF NATURAL HISTORY]

Perhaps fossils of prehistoric beasts haunt Ghost Ranch — especially the hollow, white bones of *Coelophysis*, released from the stone prison that held them for more than 200 million years. Do I sometimes hear those dry bones rattling in the canyons and across the desert?

The jacal house the Archuleta brothers built, and where Carol Stanley lived, is still in use. It has been fixed up several times and is now called Ghost House. People can visit it and get a sense of what it must have been like to live in it. (Try to imagine a grand piano in either of its small rooms.) If you are lucky you might even get to stay in an apartment that was added onto it some years ago.

From under Ghost House's eaves, the eye sockets of a sun-bleached cattle skull stare blankly toward the vast Ghost Ranch lands to the south, and Cerro Pedernal in the distance. Two giant cottonwood trees grow almost right in front of the old house. I think there is a good chance they are the very trees from which those thieves were hanged so long ago. What stories those trees could tell!

GHOST HOUSE SKULL

The first house the Packs built and Georgia O'Keeffe bought in 1940 — Rancho de los Burros — is owned by the Georgia O'Keeffe Museum and is not open to the public. The Bennett family's Casa Monte Rojo has been renamed Casa Del Sol (House of the Sun), and is used for spiritual retreats. Unfortunately, the entire area around these two historic buildings is closed to the general public, so only by taking special tours can you see them in their setting among the beautiful red and gold hills that O'Keeffe painted so often. But you can easily visit the house built by the Johnson family because, after some modification, it became the ranch's library. It is called Cottonwood and is open twenty-four hours a day.

Two newer buildings also tell stories from Ghost Ranch's past. The Ruth Hall Museum of Paleontology houses the *Coelophysis* block I mentioned earlier, and shows how it and other fossils have been discovered. A phytosaur's skeleton is displayed in a scene that depicts what the Piedra Lumbre looked like 200 million years ago. The Florence Hawley Ellis Museum of Anthropology has exhibits about human history in the area, from before the arrival of the Spanish and into the early 20th century.

Ghost Ranch today holds artifacts from and remnants of its long, sometimes frightful, but always fascinating past.

8.
The Spirit of Today's Ghost Ranch

In 1955, Arthur Pack gave Ghost Ranch to the Presbyterian Church. Since then it has been a religious, cultural, and artistic conference center for the church, as well as for people of many other religious and spiritual traditions.

In the first decades of Presbyterian ownership, many people played important roles in setting Ghost Ranch's new direction as an educational and retreat center. No person was more important in that regard than Jim Hall, Ghost Ranch's executive director from 1961 until he retired in 1986. He had the vision, the wisdom, and the determination to keep Ghost Ranch true to its long past as well as making it a welcoming place for people today. His wife, Ruth, became a fine paleontologist, and that is why the paleontology museum is named for her.

Arthur Pack wanted Ghost Ranch to be a true neighbor, not an outsider or stranger. Under Jim Hall's leadership, the Presbyterians who received the ranch continued his neighborly ways. They have been active members in the wider community, standing up for what was important to those living around them. The ranch and Hall played crucial roles in responding to the demands of Hispanic peoples in the turbulent 1960s, as well as in settling old land ownership issues in 1970s.

Today, Ghost Ranch cares for its land in ways that will ensure it is always as productive as it can be, not only for its own benefit, but also for the benefit of its neighbors. It offers workshops on Native American and Hispanic arts and crafts, and hosts mercados (markets) where beautiful jewelry, pottery, and fabric items may be purchased from the people who have made them. The bad spirits of the past have become good spirits at Ghost Ranch.

LABYRINTH AND KITCHEN MESA

Most important, unlike Rancho de los Brujos, Ghost Ranch welcomes all guests. Everything from its setting to its classes and seminars encourages people to explore new ways to express themselves and to live their lives. Here I first felt the freedom of writing what comes simply from following my heart and trusting my experience. Here, many experience a personal freedom like the freedom that mother desperately sought for herself and her child when she fled under cover of darkness. Ghost Ranch's guests today often feel the sacred Spirit of God — sometimes called the Holy Ghost — alive in very particular ways.

DINING HALL AND KITCHEN MESA AT DUSK

9.

The Spirit of Ghost Ranch in Me

This is my story of Ghost Ranch. For many, it is a magical place, just waiting to tell more tales than I could ever tell you. To me it is a place of spirit and a spiritual home. It has become an important part of my personal life story. Its spirit embraces mine.

But there is one more, deeply personal, story of Ghost Ranch that I must tell you. In the summer of 2009, my seminary classmate and long-time friend, Don Mason, fell to his death while hiking among the cliffs above the ranch. He frequently volunteered at the ranch, and was familiar with its landscape and dangers. That day, he apparently lost his way. He is memorialized at the camposanto (cemetery) not far off the trail to Box Canyon. I recall Don with both joy and sadness every time I go back. His memory is part of what Ghost Ranch means to me.

I am sure that Ghost Ranch's old ghosts are long gone, but this New Mexico desert can still give me a fright on a dark night. When the wind howls (and the coyotes, too) and the glistening stars — so bright I can see every one of them — watch me trudge up the mesa to my room, the mere thought of Ghost Ranch's many stories can send a cold shiver up my spine. I sneak a glance over my shoulder and wonder what spirit is out there, in the desert shadows, counting my every step.

I have also told you about gold, and there is gold at Ghost Ranch.

This is what I mean: often, following an afternoon thunderstorm, the most perfect rainbow arcs across the wide sky over the yellow and red cliffs. The ends of that rainbow, where legend says there are pots of gold, seem to disappear far behind those massive rock walls. When sunlight finds its way through the fleeing clouds to bathe the rainbow-framed cliffs in golden light, I think, *There's gold all over and all around and deep within those cliffs. It's a gold more precious than money; anyone who searches for it will find it.*

All it takes is a little imagination to see Ghost Ranch's gold. It has been here all the time, and it always will be.

RAINBOW OVER KITCHEN MESA

Suggested Reading

Ghosts and Gold views Ghost Ranch through my time spent there, but several fine books helped me learn its history. If you would like to know more about this wonderful place, I suggest the following, in addition to online resources:

Ghost Ranch, by Lesley Poling-Kempes (Tucson: The University of Arizona Press, 2005) is a readable, detailed history of the ranch.

We Called It Ghost Ranch, by Arthur Newton Pack (Abiquiú: Ghost Ranch Conference Center, 1966) is out of print, but used copies are available on Amazon. This excellent first-person account is well worth the search.

The Little Dinosaurs of Ghost Ranch, by Edwin H. Colbert (New York, Columbia University Press, 1995) is a first-person account of the discovery and excavation of Ghost Ranch's *Coelophysis* fossils.

Dinosaur Ghosts: The Mystery of Coelophysis, by J. Lynett Gillette (New York: Dial Books for Young Readers, 1997) explores various explanations for the deaths of so many *Coelophysis* at one time at Ghost Ranch.

Once Upon a Place: Writing from Ghost Ranch, edited by Anita Skeen and Jane Taylor (Knoxville: Night Owl Books, 2008) is a collection of essays, stories, and poems inspired by Ghost Ranch.

The Author

Keith Dean Myers (Dean) was raised among the rich farmlands of north central Iowa. Since 1989, his home has been hilly northeastern Ohio, not far from the shores of Lake Erie. He first experienced the red rock cliffs of Ghost Ranch in 1984, and has traveled to the ranch some dozen times since for seminars and workshops.

He is a graduate of Coe College (Cedar Rapids, Iowa) and of San Francisco and Pittsburgh Theological Seminaries. A retired Presbyterian minister, he has served churches in Oregon, Pennsylvania, Maryland, Illinois, and Ohio.

Dean enjoys travel in the States and beyond, reading and writing, walking and bicycling, occasionally preparing and preaching new sermons, listening to and making music, and his family and friends.

CPSIA information can be obtained
at www.ICGtesting.com
Printed in the USA
BVHW021657110520
579524BV00015B/239